Professor Bumblebrain's Bonkers Book on... JESUS

To

Hannah Calderwood

From Abernethy Church Sunday Club

2016

Published 2011 by CWR, Waverley Abbey House, Waverley Lane, Farnham, Surrey GU9 8EP, UK.
Registered Charity No. 294387. Registered Limited Company No. 1990308.

See back of book for list of National Distributors.

Editing, design and production by CWR

Printed in China by 1010 Printing International

ISBN: 978-1-85345-623-7

Professor Bumblebrain's Bonkers Book on... JESUS

ANDY ROBB

CWR

Good day to you, young person. Professor Bumblebrain's the name. Welcome to *another* of my clever and witty books. I make no apologies if that sounds a little bit big-headed. To be honest, anyone who has a brain the size of a large cabbage (as I do) is certainly going to need a whopper of a cranium in which to house the jolly thing.

You will have observed from the rather attractive cover that this book is all about **Jesus**. If you *hadn't* noticed this very obvious fact, perhaps now is the time to take a quick look before we proceed further.

If, perhaps, you have purchased this publication with the mistaken notion that it was a book on making candles out of earwax or one on how to cook ice cream on a barbecue, you are going to be **extremely disappointed**.

HOW TO MAKE CANDLES OUT OF EAR WAX BY HUGH STATIONTUBE-BLOCKAGE

I must add at this point that there are no refunds on this product (well, not from me anyway), so if you *have* made a monumental mistake in buying this book, you will simply have to grin and bear it.

Right, let us now move on.

Firstly, I would like to discover what (if anything) you know about the subject in hand, which, as we have already said, is 'Jesus'.

I have put this in the form of a test.

A spot of brisk mental stimulation will do you no harm whatsoever, young reader. May I remind you that I take examinations very seriously, so there will be no cheating, no talking and definitely no flamenco dancing. Is that clear?

Right, on with the test.

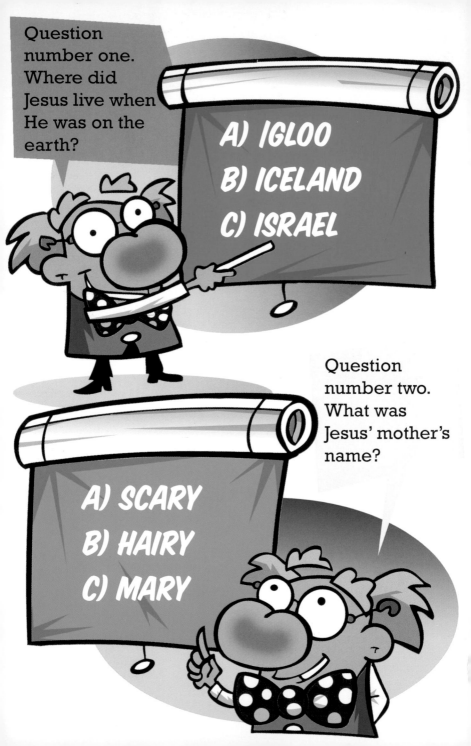

If you answered (c) for the lot of them, you can give yourself a hearty **pat on the back** for being a smarty pants.

If, on the other hand, you didn't quite get all of the answers correct ...

... then fear not, this book is tailor-made for you!

It is fair to say that most people have *some* sort of idea who Jesus is. This isn't surprising because Jesus is probably the **most famous Person** who has ever lived.

'Fraid so, Santa! But what people *think* they know about Jesus and what is actually *correct* aren't always one and the same thing, as I will now prove.

HE WAS BORN IN A STABLE, WASN'T HE?

Well, yes and no. In the familiar Christmas story (which can be found in the Bible) we are told that Jesus' mum and dad arrived at a place called **Bethlehem** shortly before their little lad was born. All correct *so* far.

Bethlehem was full of families who had returned to register themselves as part of a census (that's when all the people in a country get counted) and, as a result, there was no room for them in the inn where they had hoped to stay.

That bit is *not* quite true.

For your information, young reader, the word translated from the Greek language as **'inn'** actually can mean a *few* things, such as …

INN
-NOUN
1. A GUEST ROOM
2. AN UPPER ROOM
3. A LODGING PLACE
… AND, OF COURSE,
4. AN INN.

Which means that the innkeeper in the traditional Christmas story could *possibly* be out of a job.

THANKS A BUNCH!

Bethlehem was where Joseph's family came from, which is why *some* people now think that this 'inn' was *actually* the traditional guest room in his family's home but which was already being used by *other* relatives also visiting the town for the census, and so … there was no room at the inn, just as the Christmas story tells us.

Interesting Info

The entire New Testament part of the Bible (that's the stuff from when Jesus was born and onwards) was written in Greek. This was because Greek was the common language in those days for many countries in that region, although they still used their native languages at other times.

Anyway, back to the inn.
Probably the *only* bit of the busy house that was free would have been the ground floor, where the animals were traditionally kept, which makes sense because the Bible tells us that Jesus' mum laid her newborn baby in the animal's feeding trough (or manger) as a makeshift cot.

An interesting line of thinking, is it not?

HURUMPH! NOT TO ME IT ISN'T!

So, what *else* do you know about Jesus?

DIDN'T HE HAVE A BEARD AND LONG HAIR?

Not a clue! Nowhere in the Bible are we told what Jesus actually looked like, so *your* guess is as good as *mine*.

Er, not *exactly*, but I know what you are driving at.
A few hundred years after Jesus died, some people decided
to make His birthday the dividing point in history. Everything
before it they called **BC**, which means 'Before Christ' (that
wasn't too difficult, was it?) and everything from Jesus' birth
onwards was known as **AD** – Anno Domini (that's Latin, in case
you were wondering), which means 'in the year of our Lord'.

Funny Fact!

The date of Jesus' birth was worked out by a monk called
Dionysius Exiguus (whose name means 'Dennis the
Little') a few hundred years after the actual event.
Poor Dionysius got himself in a bit of a pickle
and ended up making a right old pig's ear of
things by miscalculating the date by a few
years. So, as ridiculous as it sounds, Jesus' birth
was more likely to have been
somewhere between **4 to 6 BC**.

If you have read any of my *other* wonderful books, one thing you will have discovered is that someone with my great intellect is able to understand things that are very likely to short-circuit the brain of a *lesser* mortal.
It is for this reason that I am somewhat reluctant to tell you my next piece of mind-boggling information, but tell you I must.

The *first* important thing to know is that Jesus is God and not just a man who lived a couple of thousand years ago. What that *means* is that before Jesus ever existed as a human being on earth, He was very much **alive and kicking** in a place called heaven.
And don't even *bother* trying to find it on Google Maps, because you won't be able to.

Jesus has *always* existed. That's because Jesus was never actually born or created (like you or me), so He's simply always been.

I *should* add that it is probably wise not to spend too long thinking about this fact. You will only end up with severe brain ache, and then *I'll* get the blame, which will not be good.

If you have read my excellent book *Professor Bumblebrain's Bonkers Book on … God*, you will be well aware that although there is only the *one* God, He consists of *three* Persons. What we have is Father God, God the Holy Spirit and, of course, the Person whom this book is all about … *Jesus* God.

You don't particularly need to try to understand this rather tricky concept, it is probably best that you simply accept it. .
One thing you do need to understand, though, is what God is like.
If there's one word that describes God above all others it is …

LOVE!

God doesn't have to *try* to love because His whole personality *is* love. That's just the way He is and that's how He's *always* been.

And because God is like this, He is always looking for something on which to shower His limitless love.

Which is why He had the brilliant idea to make you and me.

Yes, that is correct, young reader. **People** were God's brilliant idea.

If you would like to find out *more* about this interesting fact, you will have to part with your precious money and purchase a copy of my marvellous book *Professor Bumblebrain's Bonkers Book on … Creation*.

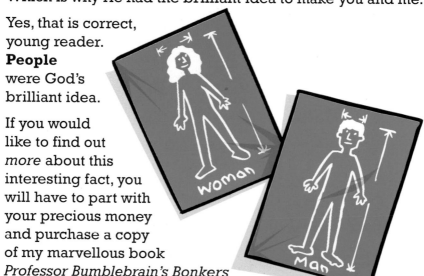

If, on the other hand, you are too stingy to do that, you'll have to be satisfied with the meagre amount of information I am about to impart. The choice is yours.

Now do stop interrupting me and let me continue.

I DIDN'T SAY ANYTHING!

Having created a wonderful world for us to live in, God topped the jolly thing off by making human beings. The plan was really quite simple. God would make creatures whom He would love, and in return they would love Him back.

Easy peasy? I am afraid not.
Sad to say, the people whom God had lovingly made decided they didn't really need God any more.

Now this was a *big* mistake.

Waiting in the wings was God's No. 1 enemy (commonly known as the devil), who took their snubbing of God as an open invitation to set up shop on Planet Earth.

The rotter couldn't have cared two hoots for the people whom God had so lovingly made. All he wanted was somewhere to strut his stuff and to **rule the roost**.

The despicable devil wasted no time in sneakily tricking people into doing things which they thought would make them happy, but in truth only ended up making things worse for them.

I'VE MADE ALL THIS MONEY AND I'M STILL NOT HAPPY!

Not only had their friendship with God been spoiled, but people also began to fall out with each other.

What a sorry mess this had all turned out to be.
God was torn.
On the one hand, He was sorry that He had ever made people.
How could they reject Him and do such horrible things to each other?

But then again, *no way* was a loving God going to give up on His wonderful creation without at least putting up a bit of a fight.

God had hit upon a brilliant plan to sort out this misery once and for all.

In pulling it off, the devil would regret the day he set foot on God's world.

Now before everyone gets carried away with excitement, there was just one itty-bitty problem with God's brilliant battle plan to restore His world back to Him, and here's what it was.

Because people had foolishly allowed the devil to slip in and to take up residence on their planet, it meant that *he* was the one who was now running the show.

And God wasn't going to just muscle in and barge that nasty piece of work out of the way. Like it or not, the devil was rightfully in charge – and I will tell you why. For this bit of the story we will have to go back to when the world was created. Not literally, of course. Not even someone with a brain the size of a large cabbage, like me, can do *that*.

The first man God made was a guy called Adam. You might well have heard of him.

HMM, THE NAME RINGS A BELL.

Adam was perfect in every way, and he and his wife (Eve) were given the awesome job of taking care of God's wonderful world.

Sad to say, they made the mistake of listening to the devil's loathsome lies and as a result ended up eating the fruit of a particular tree that God had told them was strictly out of bounds.

Their foolish disobedience was like putting out the **welcome mat** to the devil, and he certainly didn't need asking twice before coming on in and taking over things.

So, the devil was now in the driving seat and the only way things were ever going to change was for *another* perfect man (like Adam had been) to come and take back control of Planet Earth.

Although God is a loving God (as I have already informed you), He is also a just and fair God. Being just and fair means that when somebody does something right they are rewarded, but when they do something wrong they have to be punished.

HOW DO YOU PLEAD?

HOW ABOUT LIKE THIS?

Which is why, to be fair and just, all the bad things people had done (and which had spoiled God's world) needed to be punished.

There was no other choice.

For *God's* part, He made up His mind that if He could find just **one perfect human being** who would take the punishment for everybody's wrongdoing then, as far as *He* was concerned, justice would have been done.

But were there any perfect, mint-conditioned human
beings left?
Nope!
Not *one*!
The cupboard was **completely bare**.

MINT CONDITION
HUMANS

OH NO!
THEY'VE ALL
GONE!

Oh deary me. Was God's master plan about to be
scuppered before it had even got to the starting blocks?
Perish the thought!
God always knows what He is doing.

He is God after all.
As far as *God* was
concerned, it was a
no-brainer.

Jesus was going to be the
Man of the moment.
He fitted the bill perfectly
because ... well, because
He was perfect (and God!).

Now, all *Jesus* had to do was to get inside a human body, take the punishment that we deserved and it was job done! What could be more straightforward?

Well, there was the small matter of *whose* body Jesus was going to live in. He could hardly come down to earth and commandeer another person's body in the interests of saving the world, could He?

TOO RIGHT! I'M REALLY NOT TOO KEEN ON GIVING UP MY BODY QUITE YET, THANK YOU VERY MUCH!

Fear not. Jesus was going to do nothing of the sort …

PHEW! RELIEVED TO HEAR IT!

Here was the plan.
Jesus would come down to earth by being born as a baby.
Once He had a human body, He would set about sorting the rift that existed between people and God.
Isn't God smart?

YEAH, BUT HOW EXACTLY WAS GOD GOING TO PULL THIS THING OFF? SOUNDS IMPOSSIBLE TO ME.

I will tell you. In fact, I will go one better than that and I will *show* you.

You have probably had quite enough of me rambling on, so here is a jolly little comic strip about it for you to read while I pop off and make myself a well-earned cup of tea.

Happy reading and see you soon.

From the moment Adam and Eve turned their backs on God, things quickly went from bad to worse. Very soon hardly anyone gave God even a second thought, let alone worshipped Him.

It was almost as if He wasn't there.

But all was not lost.

There was one man who made it his business to keep the communication lines open between him and God, and his name was **Abram**.

AT YOUR SERVICE!

Abram (later renamed Abraham) had been told by God to 'up sticks' and go to a land called Canaan, where he was to start a family. God promised our main man that one day his family would be so large they would be as numerous as the stars in the night sky. And that's an awfully big family in anyone's book!

CANAAN

Abram's mahoosive family *eventually* became the nation of Israel. One of their leaders was a chap called Moses. You might have heard of him. God gave Moses loads of rules and laws that the Israelites had to keep to set them apart from the other naughty nations. *Some* of the rules were for their own benefit and *some* were there just to help the Israelites learn to be obedient to God. For instance …

God *then* began to give the Israelites a heads up that His Son Jesus was on the way. The hand-picked bunch of guys who delivered God's messages were called prophets, and they said things such as ...

BETHLEHEM ... THE LORD WILL CHOOSE ONE OF YOUR PEOPLE TO RULE THE NATION ...

This pinpointed the place Jesus was going to be born.

A VIRGIN IS PREGNANT, SHE WILL HAVE A SON AND WILL NAME HIM IMMANUEL (WHICH MEANS 'GOD WITH US').

This filled the people in about how Jesus was going to be born.

EVERYONE IN JERUSALEM, CELEBRATE AND SHOUT! YOUR KING HAS WON A VICTORY, AND HE IS COMING TO YOU. HE IS HUMBLE AND RIDES ON A DONKEY; HE COMES ON THE COLT OF A DONKEY.

And this message was about the build-up to the end of Jesus' life on earth.

Finally, approximately 2,000 years after Abram had stepped out in obedience to God, things began to hot up.

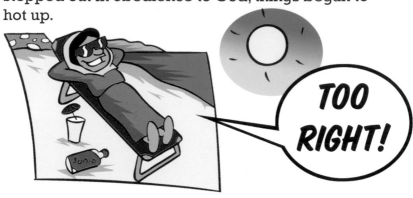

In the town of Nazareth (in Galilee) …

… a girl called Mary was minding her own business when she had a surprise visit from an angel.

LET IT HAPPEN AS YOU HAVE SAID.

God's angel was true to his word, and sure enough Mary did *indeed* have a baby boy called Jesus. In case you were wondering, God had also lined up a *human* dad for Jesus (as we mentioned earlier). His name was Joseph, and he and Mary got themselves hitched (or, if you prefer, married).

SO, THAT'S IT IN A NUTSHELL. IT WAS ANOTHER **THIRTY YEARS** BEFORE JESUS REALLY GOT CRACKING WITH THE JOB HIS FATHER IN HEAVEN HAD GIVEN HIM.

100% human

100% God

All the while Jesus made sure to live a life that was **100% pleasing to God**. How could He do that when every other human being had failed so miserably? Easy! Although Jesus was 100% human, He was also God **through and through**.

Did You Know …?

Jesus' name actually means 'God saves', which is jolly handy because that's *precisely* what Jesus had come to earth to do. To save us (or rescue us) from all the bad stuff in our lives and *also* from a life lived without being friends with God.

Are you sitting comfortably ...? ''Twas the night before Christmas, when all through the house, not a creature was stirring, not even a mouse ...'

ARE YOU SURE THAT'S FROM THE BIBLE, PROFESSOR BUMBLEBRAIN?

Oops, oh dear. Pardon me. You're right, it's not. I'm getting a little muddled. Let me begin again.

We have already heard how Mary and Joseph (Jesus' mum and dad) had arrived in Bethlehem for the census. While they waited for Jesus to pop out, so to speak, a motley bunch of shepherds were looking after their flocks in a nearby field.

Suddenly, out of the blue, an angel from God dropped by to let them know that God's Son had just been born in Bethlehem.

Before they'd had a chance to recover from this unexpected angelic visit, a whole *sky-full* of these heavenly beings rocked up to join their friend in singing songs to God.

The shepherds then hotfooted it into Bethlehem and found Jesus, just as the angel had told them.

Jesus was certainly a popular young lad, and sure enough (some time later), another group of chaps rolled up to pay Him a visit. These gents had been doing a bit of stargazing and had noticed one star that was different from all the rest.

ER, THE STAR'S OVER THERE ACTUALLY!

But there was more. As far as *these* foreign fellas were concerned, this unusual star seemed to be directing them to a **newborn king**.

After a long trek from their faraway land in the east, the men arrived in the capital city, Jerusalem, and asked to see this royal baby.

To be honest, their request didn't go down too well with the resident king (Herod) ...

So, Herod cunningly made out that he'd also like to pay a courtesy call to the boy once the visitors had tracked Him down, but between you and me the **dastardly king** wanted to do nothing of the sort. No way was there room for two kings in Herod's palace. *His* plan was to find the kid, pronto, and then to kill him.

Just to put your mind at rest, the good news is he never did.

The visitors eventually found Jesus (with the help of their handy guiding star) …

… and gave Him three special gifts of gold, frankincense and myrrh. And *that*, dear reader, ends my brief retelling of the Christmas story. Are you happy now?

Just before we leave this part of Jesus' life, you might be interested in a rather odd thing that happened as Mary and Joseph showed up at Jerusalem's Temple to offer the sacrifices to God (for their baby) that the Jewish law required.

This man (Simeon) had some other things to say about Jesus as well, about how he had been waiting for God to send someone just like Jesus. As far as *Simeon* was concerned, that day had finally arrived and he was a **happy bunny**.

As if there had not been enough surprises for Jesus' mum and dad that day, hot on Simeon's heels, an 84-year-old widow called Anna suddenly appeared. The Bible tells us that she never, ever left the Temple, and that she prayed to God 24/7. It was obvious to her that this baby was the one who'd been sent by God to save them, and she wasted no time in blabbing this to anyone who would listen.

The Bible says that after this, Jesus grew and became strong. God's blessing was on Him and He was full of wisdom.

And then the Bible goes almost completely silent about Jesus until about thirty years later.
All we get is a short story about Jesus just before He hits His teenage years.
Want to hear it?

FIRE AWAY.

Then I will tell you.

Every year, Jesus' mum and dad took a trip to Jerusalem to join their fellow Jews for the Passover Festival. Once the festival was over, they headed back home with the crowd of relatives who'd made the journey with them. Along the way, Jesus' parents were horrified to discover that their Son wasn't with them any more.

I THOUGHT YOU WERE LOOKING AFTER JESUS, JOSEPH!

DON'T BLAME ME, MARY. I HAD ENOUGH TO DO PACKING THE DONKEY.

They raced back to Jerusalem and hunted high and low for their missing lad. After a frantic **three-day search**, they eventually stumbled across Jesus in Jerusalem's Temple of all places.

What a relief to have found Him, but had Jesus been equally as anxious and worried that His parents had gone off and left Him? Nope!

In fact, they found their lad sitting down with the Jewish leaders, listening to what they had to say and quizzing them as if nothing had happened. Everyone was amazed with the smart things Jesus was saying.

WE'VE BEEN WORRIED SICK, JESUS. WHY DID YOU PUT ME AND YOUR FATHER THROUGH THIS?

WHY DID YOU HAVE TO LOOK FOR ME? DIDN'T YOU KNOW THAT I HAD TO BE IN MY FATHER'S HOUSE?

Jesus' reply flummoxed his mum and dad but, between you and me, He was talking about the fact that He was in God's Temple and God was His Father (in heaven).

I wonder if any of the Jewish leaders had the foggiest idea who Jesus *really* was?

Professor Bumblebrain's Interesting Facts ...

As we know, Joseph (Jesus' dad) was a carpenter by trade. The chances are that Jesus followed in his footsteps and learnt His dad's trade as well.

NOW HERE IS SOMETHING THAT MIGHT SURPRISE YOU. DID YOU KNOW THAT THERE ARE ADVERTS IN THE BIBLE?

ARE YOU HAVING ME ON, PROFESSOR?

Certainly not. But these aren't adverts for things like **breakfast cereal** or **comfy shoes**. They're messages that God gave to His prophets (we mentioned these guys earlier, if you were concentrating, so I'm not going to tell you about them again) to deliver to people on earth.

IT WAS GOD'S WAY OF LETTING THE WORLD KNOW THAT JESUS WAS ON HIS WAY. BUT THE MESSAGES DIDN'T END THERE.

Once Jesus had been born God had one more special messenger lined up to announce that His Son had at long last arrived on Planet Earth.
This unusual prophet's name was John the Baptist.

In case you were wondering, 'Baptist' wasn't his surname. It was just what he *did*. He baptised people.
John had been hanging out in the desert and, to tell you the truth, rather roughing it.

John baptised people (which is another word for 'dunking in water') in the nearby River Jordan as a sign that they wanted nothing more to do with all the bad stuff in their lives and that it was all going to be washed away by God ready for a **fresh start**.

One day, Jesus dropped by and asked to be baptised. Reluctantly, John agreed. Surely *God's Son* didn't need to be dunked? Hey ho! He wasn't going to argue. *Jesus* must know what He's doing even if *John* didn't.

While the pair were still in the river, a dove flew down and landed on Jesus. The Bible helpfully tells us that it was a sign that God's Holy Spirit had arrived to give Jesus the power He was going to need to carry out God's risky rescue plan.

Just to make *doubly* sure those round and about knew who Jesus was, God chipped in …

And with that, God's Holy Spirit led Jesus out into the desert for some last-minute preparation.

AS I HAVE ALREADY MENTIONED, UNLESS YOU WEREN'T PAYING ATTENTION ...

SORRY, WHAT DID YOU SAY?

... the world's first man (Adam), had made the mistake of turning his back on God and giving the devil a foothold in the world.

DO YOU HAVE TO KEEP BRINGING THAT UP?

If Jesus was going to overturn Adam's big **boo-boo**, He couldn't afford to let history repeat itself by doing the same thing.

Jesus was going to have to prove that He was up to the job, which meant Him having a **head to head** with none other than the devil himself.
If God's No. 1 enemy could succeed in tempting Jesus to do something wrong, he'd be able to stick around to continue messing things up on Planet Earth.

Ah yes, one thing I omitted to tell you was that at this point in the story, Jesus had been in the desert for **forty days** without eating.

Jesus must have been absolutely **famished**, so it should be no surprise to us that the devil's first temptation was to try and persuade Him to turn the stones on the desert floor into some yummy bread.

That ought to be no problem for God's Son, but not so fast, devil. No *way* was Jesus going to misuse the power He'd been given by God just for silly party tricks.

Jesus used words from the Jewish Scriptures to counter the devil. Jesus relied on His Father God to look after Him.

That told him.

I wonder what temptation that trickster would think up next? Here's what he came up with. He took Jesus to the highest point of Jerusalem's Temple and told Him to jump off it.

IF YOU ARE GOD'S SON, JUMP OFF. THE SCRIPTURES SAY: 'GOD WILL GIVE HIS ANGELS ORDERS ABOUT YOU. THEY WILL CATCH YOU IN THEIR ARMS, AND YOU WON'T HURT YOUR FEET ON THE STONES.'

Jesus wasn't falling for that one (apologies for my little pun). He told that time-wasting tempter to quit misusing God's Scriptures – it's not our place to test God.

The devil's *final* attempt to stop Jesus was to offer God's Son the whole world ... on *one* condition.

Would Jesus be sucked in by the devil's devious offer? Certainly not!

Interesting Info
Satan is another name the Bible uses for the devil.

AND WITH THAT, YOUNG READER, THE DEVIL SCARPERED. HURRAH! JESUS HAD PASSED THE TEST WITH FLYING COLOURS AND HE WAS NOW READY FOR ACTION.

THE FIRST THING TO DO WAS TO LET SOME PEOPLE KNOW THAT THE MESSIAH THEY'D BEEN WAITING FOR HAD FINALLY SHOWED UP.

MESSIAH

FOR THOSE OF YOU WHO DON'T KNOW, MESSIAH WAS ANOTHER NAME TO DESCRIBE WHAT JESUS WAS SENT BY GOD TO DO. JESUS WAS SPECIALLY CHOSEN BY GOD TO DO A SPECIFIC JOB.

Jesus' first port of call was the local Jewish meeting place.
They didn't have churches way back then, so if you wanted to worship God you had to go to your local **synagogue** (pronounced 'sinnergog'), and *that's* where Jesus headed.

Probably most people in Nazareth (where Jesus lived) knew the carpenter's Son, so it was a bit of surprise when, having read a chunk of Scripture which talked about God's Messiah, Jesus proceeded to drop a whopping big hint that the passage He'd just read was in fact referring to none other than *Himself*.

Was Jesus received with open arms as their Messiah? No He wasn't! To be honest, the people in the synagogue were furious with Him for saying what He did.

WHO DOES THAT YOUNG UPSTART THINK HE IS?

LET'S CHUCK HIM OVER THAT CLIFF!

Not so fast! Jesus wasn't ready to die quite so soon. Amazingly, He simply walked through the middle of the crowd to safety.

Jesus knew that if He was going to succeed in this business of patching things up between people and God, He was going to need a team to help Him. Here's how He went about getting them on board.

All together Jesus called twelve men to join Him on His rescue mission. The Bible calls them His disciples. With His trusty band of men, Jesus was finally **ready to roll** ...

AROUND THIS TIME, JESUS WENT TO A WEDDING. WITH THE CELEBRATIONS STILL IN FULL FLOW, THE WINE SUPPLY RAN OUT. **DISASTER!**

Jesus' mum (who was also there) wasted no time in volunteering her Son to sort out the problem. I'm not sure whether she had a clue what He would do, but Jesus took control of the situation and rustled up half a dozen large water jars (filled to the brim).

He told one of the servants to draw out some of the water and take it to the master of the banquet.

Of all the crazy things, the water turned into wine. But not any old wine. No sir!

When the master of the banquet took a swig, he was aghast and said to the bridegroom ...

I AM AGHAST! PEOPLE USUALLY BRING OUT THE BEST WINE FIRST AND THEN LEAVE THE CHEAPER WINE UNTIL THE GUESTS HAVE HAD TOO MUCH TO DRINK AND WON'T NOTICE. BUT YOU'VE SAVED THE BEST TILL NOW.

By now it was obvious to *everyone* that Jesus was no ordinary man and that there were definitely loads more miracles where that one came from.

Righty-ho! I think it is time for a short break while I give you a **geography-cum-history** lesson.

THAT'S HARDLY A BREAK, IS IT?

This area of land had a bit of a hard time from its neighbours, who were for ever attacking them …

... and when *Jesus* was alive, the country was *also* in the hands of the Romans, who ruled the jolly place with a rod of iron.

Much of the terrain of Israel is rocky and mountainous, which made it tricky getting from place to place.

The land also boasts two big lakes, the Dead Sea and the Sea of Galilee.

Jesus' strategy was simple. He was going to **crisscross the land** for as long as He could to let as many people know that God had come to save them. Jesus knew that there would be a time when He wasn't around any more and *then* it would be up to His twelve disciples to carry on with this rescue mission. But for *now* He had work to do.

It didn't take long for word to get out that Jesus was on the scene, and this was for two reasons.
First off, wherever Jesus went, He taught people about God in a way that nobody had ever heard before. Jesus spoke with authority.

And *second*, Jesus went around doing miracles, such as changing water into wine, healing people of their sicknesses and even bringing people back to life ...

LAZARUS, COME OUT!

So, how about we take a look at some of the amazing things that Jesus said and *then* we'll look at some more of His awesome miracles and healings. How does that sound?

GO FOR IT!

Some things Jesus said ...

YOU HAVE HEARD PEOPLE SAY, 'LOVE YOUR NEIGHBOURS AND HATE YOUR ENEMIES.' BUT I TELL YOU TO LOVE YOUR ENEMIES AND PRAY FOR ANYONE WHO ILL-TREATS YOU.

I LOVE YOU.

I LOVE YOU TOO.

One night, one of the Jewish religious leaders paid Jesus a secret visit. These guys had been running the show for centuries and most of the time their petty man-made rules had made it next to impossible for ordinary folk to get to know God.

Jesus hadn't got time for all that stuff.
This made Him a big hit with the crowds but it made
Him the enemy of most of the religious leaders.

The man who turned up for this secret meeting in the dead of night was a chap called Nicodemus. He was a bit more sympathetic to Jesus than the rest and wanted to find out more about Him.

SIR, WE KNOW THAT GOD HAS SENT YOU TO TEACH US. YOU COULD NOT PERFORM THESE MIRACLES, UNLESS GOD WERE WITH YOU.

I TELL YOU FOR CERTAIN THAT YOU MUST BE BORN FROM ABOVE BEFORE YOU CAN SEE GOD'S KINGDOM.

HOW CAN A GROWN MAN EVER BE BORN A SECOND TIME?

GOD LOVED THE PEOPLE OF THIS WORLD SO MUCH THAT HE GAVE HIS ONLY SON, SO THAT EVERYONE WHO HAS FAITH IN HIM WILL HAVE ETERNAL LIFE AND NEVER REALLY DIE.

OH, I THINK I GET IT! I GET A NEW START IN LIFE WHEN I PUT MY TRUST IN YOU ...

Sometimes Jesus told short stories to get His message across, like this one about a couple of men who both built themselves a house.

One of them very sensibly erected his property on firm, rocky ground, but the other one was not *quite* so smart.

He built his property on sand, and I'll let Jesus take up the story from there ...

RAIN POURED DOWN, RIVERS FLOODED, AND WINDS BEAT AGAINST THAT HOUSE. BUT IT DID NOT FALL, BECAUSE IT WAS BUILT ON SOLID ROCK. ANYONE WHO HEARS MY TEACHINGS AND DOESN'T OBEY THEM IS LIKE A FOOLISH PERSON WHO BUILDS A HOUSE ON SAND. THE RAIN POURED DOWN, THE RIVERS FLOODED, AND THE WINDS BLEW AND BEAT AGAINST THAT HOUSE. FINALLY, IT FELL WITH A CRASH.

And that ends my rather brief dip into some of the many fascinating things Jesus had to say.

Not only was Jesus a brilliant teacher, but *also* He was a bit of an **action Man**, so let's take a look at some of the awesome things He did.

If you have been paying attention, you will remember I told you that Jesus had been filled with Holy Spirit power.

I WAS ACTUALLY!

This wasn't so He could beat up His enemies. No, Jesus chose to use His God-given power to do good things to demonstrate to people that God loved them and cared for them.

One day, Jesus was down by the shore of Lake Galilee when a man called Jairus flung himself at Jesus' feet and begged for His help.

The poor man's daughter was seriously ill and was in danger of dying at any moment.

> **MY DAUGHTER IS ABOUT TO DIE! PLEASE COME AND TOUCH HER, SO SHE WILL GET WELL AND LIVE.**

As the crowd pressed in to see what Jesus would do, a sick woman pushed her way through and reached out her hand to touch Jesus' cloak. For years the poor lady had suffered with bleeding, but suddenly it stopped ... just like that!

> **WHO TOUCHED MY CLOTHES?**

> **WHAT A WEIRD QUESTION. LOADS OF PEOPLE ARE TOUCHING OUR MASTER.**

Jesus wasn't stupid. He knew that. What Jesus *meant* was that He felt the power that was in Him flow out to the sick woman and heal her.

Wow!

Was Jesus mad at the woman?

No, of *course* He wasn't!
Jesus praised the lady
for putting her trust
in Him.
Now back to Jairus.

Oh deary me!
It looks like we're too late ...

Some people might have given up on the little girl, but Jesus wasn't the least bit fazed by this piece of bad news.

Jesus simply told Jairus not to be afraid and to put His faith in God.

When they arrived at Jairus' house, the place was filled with the weeping and wailing of grieving friends and relatives.

Jesus was having none of it. It wasn't that He was hard-hearted, just the fact that no way was He going to give up on the girl quite so easily and their noise was a distraction. Jesus cleared the lot of them out of the house and, with her parents and His disciples in tow, went in to see the girl.

LITTLE GIRL, GET UP!

IT'S A MIRACLE!

Another time Jesus was out and about teaching and healing people when His disciples suddenly realised that it was getting late and that the huge crowd following their Master around were hungry and in need of food.

Jesus was always on the lookout for ways to help His team learn to trust in God more, so He said …

What I *forgot* to tell you was that there were about 5,000 men ready and waiting for a slap-up meal, and that *didn't* include all the women and children who don't even get a mention in the Bible accounts of this amazing story.

What we could *possibly* be looking at here is a whopping 10,000 hungry mouths to feed!

This might have panicked Jesus' disciples, but He wasn't in the least bit worried. Jesus took five loaves and two fishes, which a young lad had kindly donated, thanked God for the food and set about passing it round to the famished crowd.

I DON'T THINK IT'S GONNA STRETCH VERY FAR.

Jesus had the crowd sit down on the grass and then ordered His disciples to distribute the boy's packed lunch. Did the food run out? It didn't. Here's the miracle. Everyone had enough to eat and there were even leftovers.

Twelve baskets full to be precise. That was one for each disciple.

Let me give you one *last* example of what Jesus' awesome power can do.

One day, Jesus and His trusty band of men were heading out across a lake in a boat when, without warning, a rather nasty storm blew up.

In the meantime, Jesus had nodded off to sleep.

Jesus didn't seem in the least bit bothered by the waves crashing into the boat.

And with that the storm stopped.

The disciples were completely freaked out by the whole thing.

AFTER MORE THAN THREE HECTIC YEARS OF TRAVELLING TO AND FRO ACROSS THE LAND, PREACHING AND HEALING PEOPLE, THE TIME HAD FINALLY COME FOR THE HARDEST PART OF ALL.

It was *one* thing telling people they needed to turn back to God, but without someone to take the punishment for all the wrong stuff in their lives, they were never going to be able to be friends with God. Jesus knew full well what had to be done to finish the job, and so He began to make tracks for Jerusalem for the **big finale** to His time on earth.

JESUS HAD IT ALL PLANNED OUT. NOTHING WOULD HAPPEN BY ACCIDENT.

Jesus was approaching the capital city, Jerusalem, just as the Jewish Passover Festival was about to begin.
During this celebration, the Jews thanked God for rescuing them from slavery in Egypt.

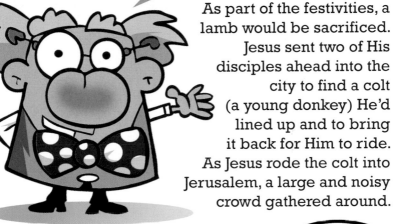

As part of the festivities, a lamb would be sacrificed. Jesus sent two of His disciples ahead into the city to find a colt (a young donkey) He'd lined up and to bring it back for Him to ride. As Jesus rode the colt into Jerusalem, a large and noisy crowd gathered around.

It was no coincidence – Jesus was showing us loud and clear that He was going to be the lamb sacrificed in order to bring us back to God.

The **riled religious leaders** were none too happy about the disturbance that Jesus' entry into the city was causing, but there was little they could do to stop it.

The religious leaders might have hated Jesus' guts, but because the crowds adored Him they could do nothing to harm Him. They'd just have to bide their time until the right moment.

I REALLY DON'T KNOW HOW MUCH LONGER I CAN KEEP UP THIS 'BIDING MY TIME' THING!

As part of the Passover Festival, the Jews always shared a special meal together.

THIS WAS GOING TO BE THE LAST TIME JESUS ATE WITH HIS DISCIPLES BEFORE HE MET HIS END, SO HE HAD ARRANGED FOR A ROOM TO BE SPECIALLY PREPARED FOR THIS VERY PURPOSE. TO EVERYONE'S ASTONISHMENT, JESUS DIDN'T DO THINGS THE TRADITIONAL WAY.

When the time came to eat the Passover bread, Jesus broke it and then said …

TAKE THIS AND EAT IT. THIS IS MY BODY.

Was the penny starting to drop that their Master was going to die? Next up, Jesus passed round the wine.

THIS IS MY BLOOD … POURED OUT, SO THAT MANY PEOPLE WILL HAVE THEIR SINS FORGIVEN.

Did You Know …?
'Sin' is a word the Bible uses to describe bad stuff we do which separates us from God. *Now* you know!

Back to the story. In the middle of this final meal, Jesus dropped a **big bombshell** …

ONE OF YOU WILL BETRAY ME.

IT DIDN'T TAKE LONG TO DISCOVER WHO THE DOUBLE-CROSSER WAS.

While the rest of the disciples were wondering if it would be them, Judas (their thieving treasurer) raced from the room and out into the night.

For whatever reason, Judas hadn't been happy with how things were going and he'd taken a backhander of **thirty silver coins** from the Jewish religious leaders in exchange for telling them where they could arrest Jesus, far away from the adoring crowds.

Jesus knew that His time on earth was now short and He went into a garden outside Jerusalem with His disciples to pray to God for the strength to go through with His heroic rescue mission.

To carry the weight of the world's sin was going to be mighty costly to Jesus, and just the *thought* of it was becoming almost too much to bear.

I AM SO SAD THAT I FEEL AS IF I AM DYING. STAY HERE AND KEEP AWAKE WITH ME.

While Jesus carried on praying, His disciples drifted off to sleep ... but not for long. They were rudely awoken from their slumbers by the arrival of Judas and the marauding mob who had come along with him to arrest Jesus.

Judas immediately made a beeline for Jesus and identified Him to his accomplices with a kiss.

The dirty deed was done.

Jesus was forcibly led away to the high priest's house to be cross-examined, while the scaredy-cat disciples made themselves scarce. The religious leaders did not like Jesus one jot and they were going to do their very best to stitch Him up good and proper, one way or the other.

As far as *they* were concerned, the sooner this 'Messiah Man' was out of the way the better.

THIS MAN CLAIMED THAT HE WOULD TEAR DOWN GOD'S TEMPLE AND BUILD IT AGAIN IN THREE DAYS.

What Jesus *meant* was that He was going to die and then come to life again after three days, but His accusers weren't interested in Jesus' explanations.

The religious leaders had no intention of executing Jesus themselves. Their plan was for the Roman governor (Pontius Pilate) to carry out the dastardly deed for them.
Not only that, but they *also* wanted Jesus dealt with pretty sharpish, before their fast-approaching Jewish Sabbath (their day of rest) began.

Jesus was brought before the governor to be questioned.

Much to Pilate's frustration, Jesus remained **tight-lipped** and wouldn't answer his questions. It quite quickly became obvious to Pontius Pilate that Jesus was completely innocent of any crime (other than of getting right up the noses of the religious leaders), so he tried to concoct a way to set Him free.

The governor had a custom to release a prisoner each Passover. No doubt he'd heard that Jesus was popular with the people and probably banked on them asking for Him to be released. That would solve all his problems and get those annoying religious leaders off his back.
Not so!
What Pilate hadn't bargained on was the rotten religious leaders stirring up a crowd to call for a murderer called Barabbas to be freed instead. How infuriating was *that*?

Pilate was powerless to do *anything* and Jesus was led away by the Roman soldiers to be executed.

The soldiers had an absolute field day with Jesus, pressing a painful crown of thorns onto His head and draping a robe around His shoulders to take the mickey out of Him because He claimed to be King of the Jews. Little did they realise He really *was*.

The Romans were absolute experts at executing people, and one of their cruellest methods was that of **crucifixion**. This involved being nailed by your hands and feet to a wooden cross and then being left hanging there until you were dead.

TOO MUCH INFORMATION!

Did You Know …?

The word 'EXCRUCIATING', used to describe terrible pain, actually comes from the act of crucifying someone.

As Jesus hung on the cross in the heat of the day, the Roman soldiers below gambled for His clothing and passers-by shouted cruel taunts at Him.

Mary, Jesus' mum, watched from a distance, helpless to stop what was happening to her beloved Son.

Then, at midday, a mysterious darkness covered the whole country and lasted for a **terrifying three hours**.

COULD IT BE THAT IT WAS GOD'S WAY OF SHOWING THE WORLD JUST HOW MUCH HIS ONE AND ONLY SON WAS SUFFERING FOR THEM? WHO KNOWS?

AND THEN, WITH HIS LAST BREATH, JESUS CRIED OUT AT THE TOP OF HIS VOICE, 'IT IS FINISHED!' AND, WITH THAT, HE DIED. ALL OF A SUDDEN WEIRD THINGS BEGAN TO HAPPEN.

The city was rocked by a frightening earthquake …

The massive curtain in Jerusalem's Temple split from top to bottom (as a sign that people and God could now be friends) …

And the graves of dead people opened up and their inhabitants began to wander around the city.

I'M BACK!

That evening, a rich man called Joseph went to see Pontius Pilate to ask if he could take Jesus' body away for a proper burial.
The governor agreed to the request.

Jesus was laid in a tomb and a large stone was rolled across its entrance.

For all the strange goings on, it seemed as though that was the end of Jesus.

Or *was* it?

You'd have thought the religious leaders would be clicking their heels with joy at the thought of finally having Jesus out of the way but, come the next day, they were beginning to feel rather uneasy.

Sure, Jesus was dead and they'd got their wicked way, but somehow they couldn't seem to shake the thought of Jesus' comment about Him coming back to life in three days' time.

The religious leaders really couldn't afford to take any chances, so a guard was hastily placed at the entrance to the tomb to prevent anything untoward taking place.

Because of their traditions, the Jews were forbidden from doing very much on their Sabbath day, so it wasn't until early Sunday morning (on the third day after Jesus' death) that a group of women showed up at the tomb to cover Jesus' body with ritual spices.

When they arrived on the scene, the women were surprised to discover that the stone covering the entrance to the tomb had been rolled away by an angel, who was sitting on it as if he was waiting for them.

DON'T BE AFRAID! I KNOW YOU ARE LOOKING FOR JESUS, WHO WAS NAILED TO A CROSS. HE ISN'T HERE! GOD HAS RAISED HIM TO LIFE, JUST AS JESUS SAID HE WOULD.

God had brought Jesus back to life.

The women hurried back to tell Jesus' disciples the good news. Two of the disciples (Peter and John) raced to the tomb to see if what the women were saying was really true.

It sure was!

But here's something that is even more astounding.

Not only was Jesus not dead any more, but loads and loads of His followers actually got to see Him alive again over the next forty days.

One of these was a lady called Mary, who had been one of Jesus' followers. She met Jesus near the tomb and mistakenly presumed He was the gardener until He gently put her straight.

Another time Jesus appeared to some of His disciples while they were meeting together in a locked room. They were overjoyed to see Jesus, but when they told Thomas (one of the Twelve who hadn't been there at the time), he wasn't quite sure whether to believe their tale or not.

Only when Jesus made a return visit especially for Thomas and he saw the scars in Jesus' hands where He'd been nailed to the cross, did Thomas cotton on to the fact that his Master was **very much alive**, just as he'd been told.

MY LORD AND MY GOD!

Jesus said that it was all well and good *saying* you believed in Him when you could see Him face to face, but full marks to anybody who put their trust in Him when they hadn't had that luxury. He was meaning people like you and me, who weren't around 2,000 years ago.

After His resurrection, Jesus spent forty days with His disciples, and in that time the Bible says that over 500 people saw Him **alive and well**. How amazing is *that*? Finally, it was time for Jesus to return home to heaven.

Jesus had left His followers in no doubt whatsoever that He had succeeded in His mission and that He really was who He said He was.

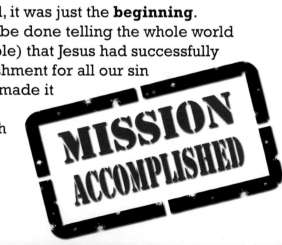

HE'S THE SON OF GOD WHO CAME TO SAVE US.

And so Jesus led His group of close friends outside the city and said His last farewells.

But as far as Jesus was concerned, this wasn't a time for tears.

This wasn't the end, it was just the **beginning**.

There was work to be done telling the whole world (not just their people) that Jesus had successfully taken the full punishment for all our sin and that Jesus had made it possible for us to have a new life with Him.

Just as He'd told Nicodemus.

It was …

MISSION ACCOMPLISHED

But before the disciples were let loose to **spill the beans**, they were going to need God's power inside them so they could do the job properly.

Remember when Jesus received the Holy Spirit's power before He began doing His amazing stuff?

Well, that's what *these* guys were going to need as well.

DON'T LEAVE JERUSALEM YET. WAIT HERE FOR THE FATHER TO GIVE YOU THE HOLY SPIRIT.

Shortly after this, Jesus was taken up to heaven before their very eyes.

While the disciples stared up into the sky, open mouthed, a couple of angels showed up ...

WHY ARE YOU MEN FROM GALILEE STANDING HERE AND LOOKING UP INTO THE SKY? JESUS HAS BEEN TAKEN TO HEAVEN. BUT HE WILL COME BACK IN THE SAME WAY THAT YOU HAVE SEEN HIM GO.

It was Jesus' world to start with and He is coming back to rule over it for ever.

He will not only remove everything bad, once and for all, but Jesus will *also* make a completely new heaven and a new earth for those who love Him to enjoy forever.

It'll be like it was at the beginning of time when God and humans had the pleasure of each other's company on the planet.

God the Father was pleased that His precious Son had made it possible for us to be His friends once again. Because of that, God didn't just have *one* Son, He now had *countless* children to share for ever with.

The Bible says that **Jesus** is the only way to get back to being friends with God.

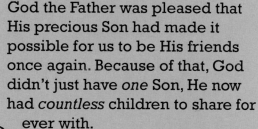

You can read your Bible regularly. You can pray and go to church. You can give your money to poor people but, as hard as you might try, there is absolutely nothing you can do to make yourself right in the eyes of God.

Don't get me wrong, young reader. God most certainly gives the big thumbs up to all the things just mentioned, but only *Jesus* is capable of removing our sin. *Our* job is simply to believe that He has done that for us.

It's like a precious gift from God.

We can't do a thing to earn it, so the best we can do is to say a hearty ...

THANK YOU, JESUS!

The Bible says that if you really believe Jesus is God's Son sent to rescue us and that He did all the things we have looked at in this book, *you too* can be a friend of God (that's if you're not already).

Jesus spent a lot of time talking to His Father in heaven (the Bible calls this praying), and you can talk to God about becoming His friend right now if you would like.

IF YOU'RE NOT QUITE SURE WHAT TO SAY TO GOD, HERE'S A SUGGESTION.

Dear God,
Forgive me for the bad things I have done in my life, for living my way and not Your way. Thank You that You sent Jesus to earth to take the punishment for all these bad things and that He rose to life again to give me life. I give my life to You and ask that You will fill me with Your Holy Spirit, just as You did the disciples, so that from now on I can live a life that pleases You. Amen.

Well, that is about it for this book. I hope that you have found it both **instructive** and **helpful**. If you *did* pray that prayer, do be sure to let another Christian know about it so that they can really encourage you. And don't let that be the last time you talk to God.

Keep on praying every day.

Now that you are friends with God, make it your **top priority** to get to know Him really well.
Also get your hands on a Bible (if you haven't already) and start to read up some more about God and Jesus.

I DO HOPE THIS BOOK HAS NOT BEEN TOO TAXING ON YOUR GREY CELLS, YOUNG READER - AFTER ALL, NOT EVERYONE HAS A BRAIN THE SIZE OF A LARGE CABBAGE, AS I DO!

National Distributors

UK: (and countries not listed below)
CWR, Waverley Abbey House, Waverley Lane, Farnham, Surrey GU9 8EP.
Tel: (01252) 784700 Outside UK (44) 1252 784700 Email: mail@cwr.org.uk

AUSTRALIA: KI Entertainment, Unit 21 317-321 Woodpark Road, Smithfield, New South Wales 2164.
Tel: 1 800 850 777 Fax: 02 9604 3699 Email: sales@kientertainment.com.au

CANADA: David C Cook Distribution Canada, PO Box 98, 55 Woodslee Avenue, Paris,
Ontario N3L 3E5. Tel: 1800 263 2664 Email: sandi.swanson@davidccook.ca

GHANA: Challenge Enterprises of Ghana, PO Box 5723, Accra. Tel: (021) 222437/223249
Fax: (021) 226227 Email: ceg@africaonline.com.gh

HONG KONG: Cross Communications Ltd, 1/F, 562A Nathan Road, Kowloon.
Tel: 2780 1188 Fax: 2770 6229 Email: cross@crosshk.com

INDIA: Crystal Communications, 10-3-18/4/1, East Marredpalli, Secunderabad – 500026, Andhra Pradesh.
Tel/Fax: (040) 27737145 Email: crystal_edwj@rediffmail.com

KENYA: Keswick Books and Gifts Ltd, PO Box 10242-00400, Nairobi.
Tel: (254) 20 312639/3870125 Email: keswick@swiftkenya.com

MALAYSIA: Canaanland, No. 25 Jalan PJU 1A/41B, NZX Commercial Centre, Ara Jaya, 47301 Petaling Jaya,
Selangor. Tel: (03) 7885 0540/1/2 Fax: (03) 7885 0545 Email: info@canaanland.com.my

Salvation Book Centre (M) Sdn Bhd, 23 Jalan SS 2/64, 47300 Petaling Jaya, Selangor.
Tel: (03) 78766411/78766797 Fax: (03) 78757066/78756360
Email: info@salvationbookcentre.com

NEW ZEALAND: KI Entertainment, Unit 21 317-321 Woodpark Road, Smithfield,
New South Wales 2164, Australia. Tel: 0 800 850 777 Fax: +612 9604 3699
Email: sales@kientertainment.com.au

NIGERIA: FBFM, Helen Baugh House, 96 St Finbarr's College Road, Akoka, Lagos.
Tel: (01) 7747429/4700218/825775/827264 Email: fbfm@hyperia.com

PHILIPPINES: OMF Literature Inc, 776 Boni Avenue, Mandaluyong City.
Tel: (02) 531 2183 Fax: (02) 531 1960 Email: gloadlaon@omflit.com

SINGAPORE: Alby Commercial Enterprises Pte Ltd, 95 Kallang Avenue #04-00, AIS Industrial Building, 339420.
Tel: (65) 629 27238 Fax: (65) 629 27235 Email: marketing@alby.com.sg

SOUTH AFRICA: Struik Christian Books, 80 MacKenzie Street, PO Box 1144, Cape Town 8000.
Tel: (021) 462 4360 Fax: (021) 461 3612 Email: info@struikchristianmedia.co.za

SRI LANKA: Christombu Publications (Pvt) Ltd, Bartleet House, 65 Braybrooke Place, Colombo 2.
Tel: (9411) 2421073/2447665 Email: dhanad@bartleet.com

USA: David C Cook Distribution Canada, PO Box 98, 55 Woodslee Avenue, Paris, Ontario N3L 3E5, Canada.
Tel: 1800 263 2664 Email: sandi.swanson@davidccook.ca

CWR is a Registered Charity - Number 294387
CWR is a Limited Company registered in England - Registration Number 1990308

IF YOU LIKED THIS BOOK YOU'LL LOVE THE BARMY PROFESSOR'S OTHER STORIES BY ANDY ROBB

Professor Bumblebrain's Bonkers Book on Bible Heroes
At the Professor's exciting award ceremony, The Bumblebrains,
we're introduced to a star-studded line-up.
ISBN: 978-1-85345-578-0

Professor Bumblebrain's Bonkers Book on Creation
Join Professor Bumblebrain as he helps you look at ideas concerning the
start of the world, how amazing we humans are, and whether the universe
is all God's handiwork.
ISBN: 978-1-85345-622-0

Professor Bumblebrain's Bonkers Book on God
Get the Professor's brainy answers to questions like Who is God?
What is He like? Where does He live? How can I get to know Him?
ISBN: 978-1-85345-579-7

100-page paperbacks, 129x197mm

More from Andy Robb!

The Bible is not an easy book to understand if you don't know where to start.

That's why Andy Robb has picked out some of the most exciting stories for you and told them in his own wacky way – which certainly won't leave you bored!

Each story has a cliffhanger ending – and a short Bible passage to look up so you can find out what happened next.

112-page paperbacks, 197x129mm

50 Goriest Bible Stories
Cain and Abel, Abraham and Isaac, Moses and his rebellious relations, David and Goliath, Judas and more.
ISBN: 978-1-85345-530-8

50 Weirdest Bible Stories
The Red Sea crossing, Jesus heals a paralysed man, manna in the desert, the dreams of Joseph, Peter walking on water and more.
ISBN: 978-1-85345-489-9

50 Wildest Bible Stories
Ruth and Boaz, Samson killing a lion with his bare hands, the Queen of Sheba's visit to Solomon, Jesus' temptation by Satan, Paul's angelic visit onboard a ship and more.
ISBN: 978-1-85345-529-2

50 Craziest Bible Stories
Jonah and the big fish, Elijah and the prophets of Baal, Balaam and the donkey, the feeding of the 5,000, Jesus' resurrection, the beggar at the Beautiful Gate and more.
ISBN: 978-1-85345-490-5

For current prices visit www.cwr.org.uk/store
Also available at your local Christian bookshop